ELECTRO-CHROMATIC
An EDM Coloring Book Journey

Jadie Press

This Coloring Book Belongs To:

____

Electro-Chromatic

Electro-Chromatic

Electro-Chromatic

Electro-Chromatic

Electro-Chromatic

Electro-Chromatic

Electro-Chromatic

Electro-Chromatic

Electro-Chromatic

Electro-Chromatic

Electro-Chromatic

Electro-Chromatic

Electro-Chromatic

Electro-Chromatic

Electro-Chromatic

Electro-Chromatic

Electro-Chromatic

Electro-Chromatic

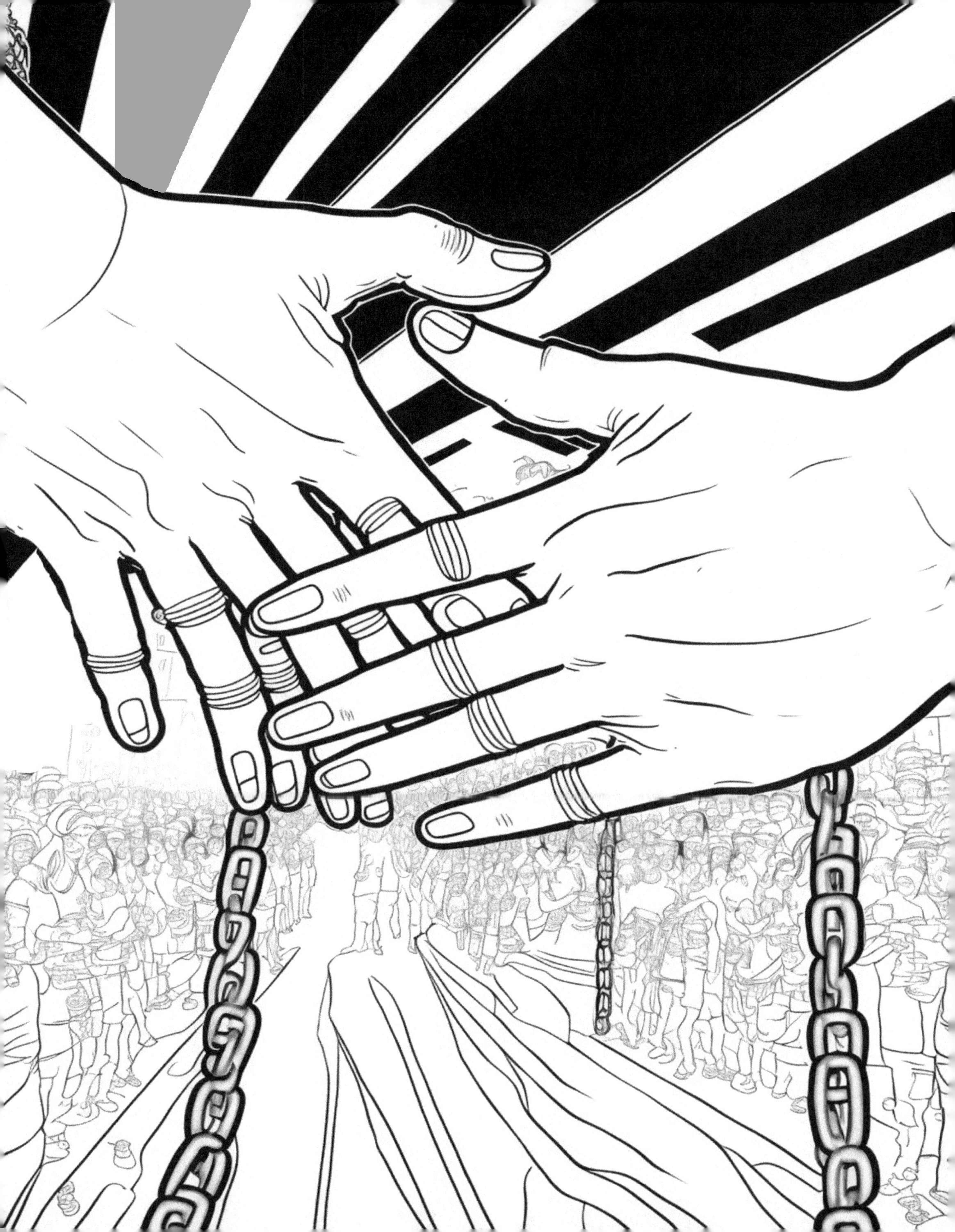

Electro-Chromatic

Electro-Chromatic

Electro-Chromatic

Electro-Chromatic

Electro-Chromatic

Electro-Chromatic

Electro-Chromatic

Electro-Chromatic

Electro-Chromatic

Electro-Chromatic

Electro-Chromatic

Electro-Chromatic

Electro-Chromatic

Electro-Chromatic

Electro-Chromatic

Electro-Chromatic

Electro-Chromatic

Electro-Chromatic

Electro-Chromatic

Electro-Chromatic

FAYG

Electro-Chromatic

Electro-Chromatic

Electro-Chromatic

Electro-Chromatic

Electro-Chromatic

Electro-Chromatic

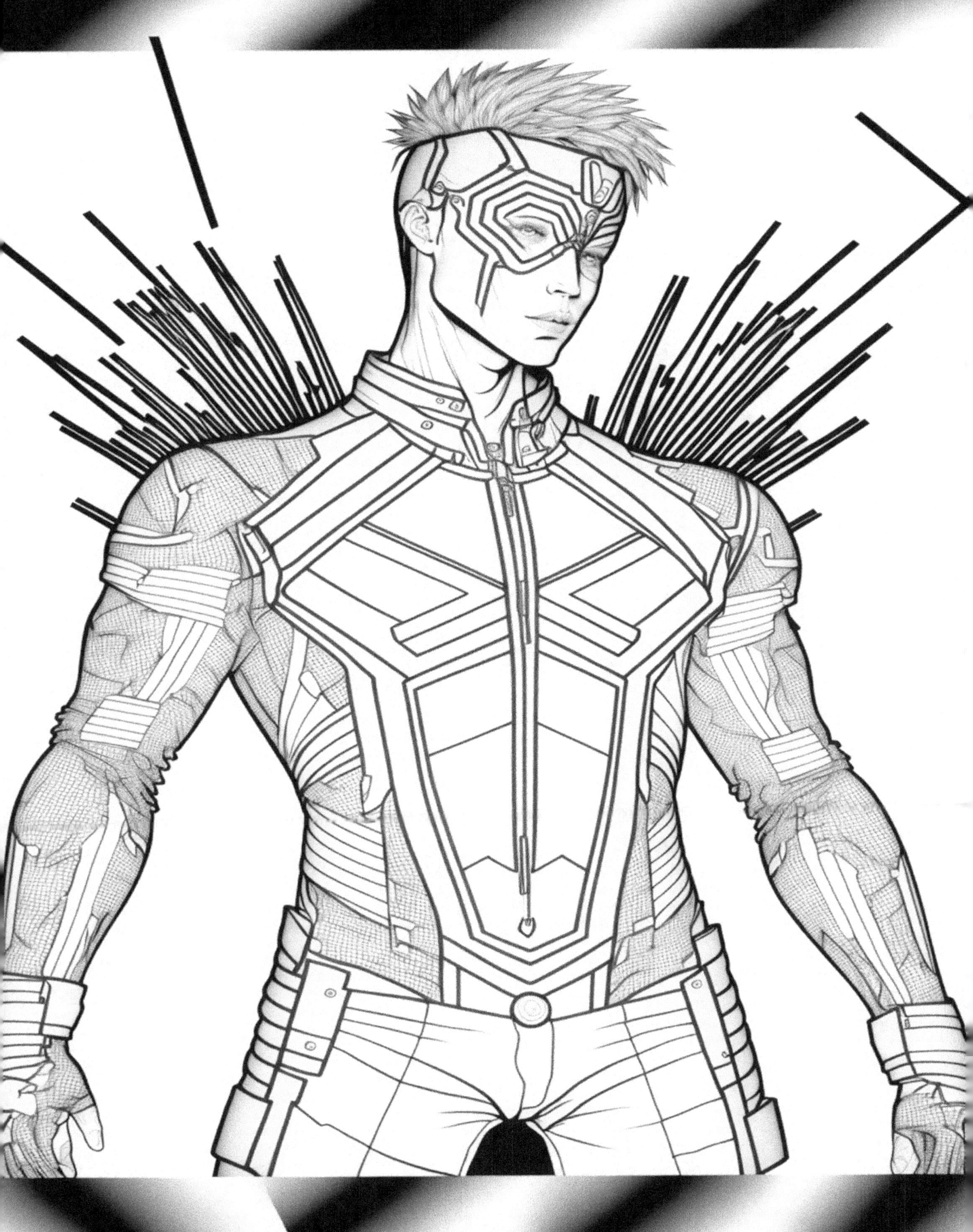

Electro-Chromatic

Electro-Chromatic

Electro-Chromatic

Electro-Chromatic

Electro-Chromatic

Electro-Chromatic

Electro-Chromatic

Electro-Chromatic

Electro-Chromatic

Electro-Chromatic

Electro-Chromatic

Electro-Chromatic

Electro-Chromatic